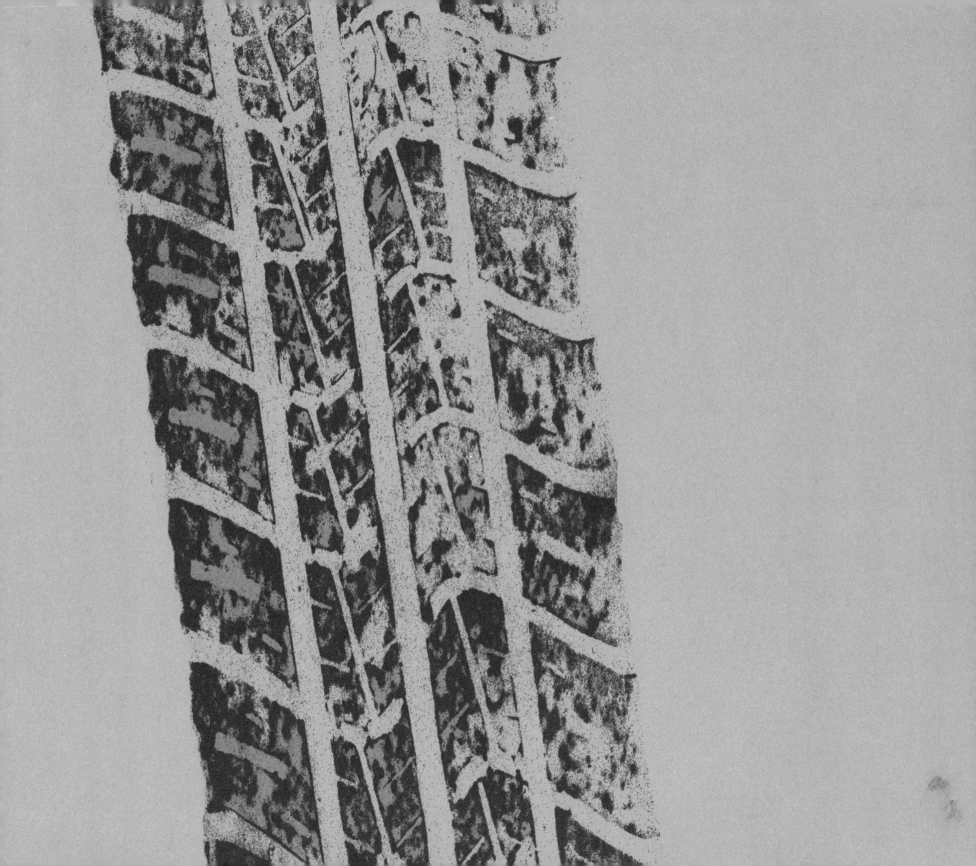

I DRIVE A SNOWPLOW

by **Sarah Bridges**

illustrated by **Derrick Alderman** & **Denise Shea**

PICTURE WINDOW BOOKS
Minneapolis, Minnesota

Managing Editors: Bob Temple, Catherine Neitge
Creative Director: Terri Foley
Editors: Brenda Haugen, Christianne Jones
Editorial Adviser: Andrea Cascardi
Designer: Nathan Gassman
Storyboard development: Amy Bailey Muehlenhardt
Page production: Banta Digital Group
The illustrations in this book were rendered digitally.

Picture Window Books
5115 Excelsior Boulevard
Suite 232
Minneapolis, MN 55416
877-845-8392
www.picturewindowbooks.com

Printed in the United States of America.

Library of Congress Cataloging-in-Publication Data
Bridges, Sarah.
I drive a snowplow / by Sarah Bridges ; illustrated by Derrick
    Alderman and Denise Shea.
p. cm. — (Working wheels)
Includes bibliographical references and index.
ISBN 1-4048-0617-2 (reinforced library binding : alk. paper)
1. Snowplows—Juvenile literature. [1. Snowplows.] I. Alderman,
    Derrick, ill. II. Shea, Denise, ill. III. Title. IV. Series.
TD868.B75 2004
625.7'63—dc22   2003028229

Thanks to Rob at the Minnesota Department of Transportation for the snowplow lessons—S.B.

Thanks to our advisers for their expertise, research, and advice:

Tom Colbert, P.E., Public Works Director
Eagan, Minnesota

Susan Kesselring, M.A., Literacy Educator
Rosemount-Apple Valley-Eagan (Minnesota) School District

My name is Nicole,
and I drive a snowplow.

4

Before I start work,
I check the vehicle's
brakes, snowplow blade,
and tires. I also clean
the mirrors.

Each snowplow has six mirrors.
They help the driver see what is
around the vehicle.

My vehicle is really a dump truck with
a snowplow blade hooked on the front.
The box in the back is filled with
sand and salt.

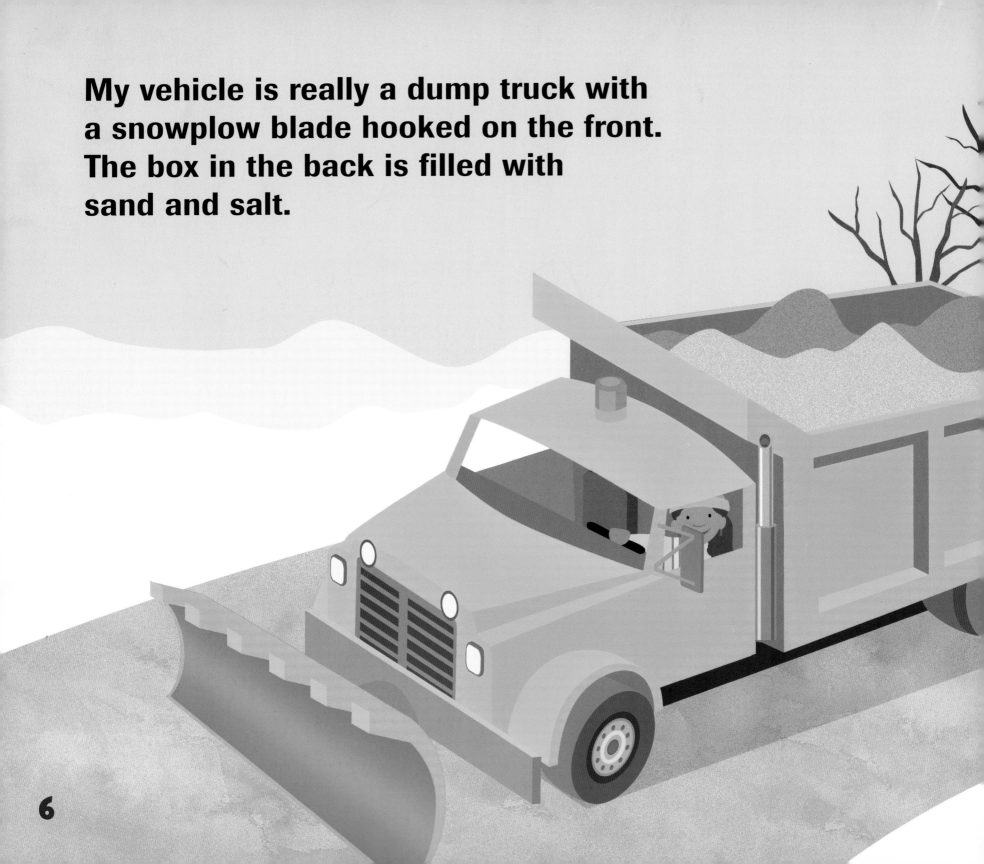

Salt is used to melt the snow and ice. Sand is used to make the roads less _slippery_.

The salt and sand piles are stored in covered sheds to keep them dry. The salt and sand will turn into giant blocks if they get wet.

My truck is taller than a basketball hoop. I climb up three steps to get into the cab.

I can look down on all the other cars from my cab.

A snowplow is one of the biggest vehicles on the road. When it is full of sand and salt, a snowplow weighs about 50,000 pounds (22,500 kilograms)!

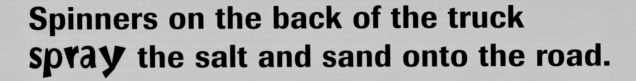

Spinners on the back of the truck **spray** the salt and sand onto the road.

The spinners are plastic disks that whirl in a circle. The faster the spinners turn, the more salt and sand they spray on the road.

My snowplow has special dials inside. The dials change the amount of sand and salt I dump.

11

I make the snowplow blade move by using a joystick.

12

I can make the blade go up, down, and sideways.

An average snowplow blade is 12 feet (3.6 meters) wide. Some plows also have a wing blade. The wing blade adds another 10 feet (3 meters) to the right side of the plow.

13

My snowplow has a **flashing** light that helps people see me in bad weather. The light sits on top of the cab.

A snowplow also has red-and-white tape that glistens when a car's headlights shine on it.

My snowplow's main job is to push snow off the road.

When I lower my blade to start work, it hits the ground with a *crash*. Sometimes *sparks* even fly when I'm driving over the hard pavement!

Bridges and overpasses are cleared by giant snowblowers. They can't be cleared by snowplows because the snow would fall on the cars below.

17

My truck works in very bad weather. I must drive slowly for safety. I drive about 25 miles per hour.

Other cars must stay far behind me. I can't see them if they get too close. Once a car hit my fender, and I didn't even feel it because my snowplow is so big!

Drivers should move with caution around a snowplow. The extra lights and other safety features on a snowplow help warn other drivers.

19

After I clear all the roads, I go back to the garage to clean my snowplow.

I drive the truck through a washer. Now the snowplow is clean and ready for the next trip.

In one 12-hour shift, snowplows use about 55 gallons (200 liters) of fuel. The driver always makes sure the tank is full before taking the snowplow out.

SNOWPLOW DIAGRAM

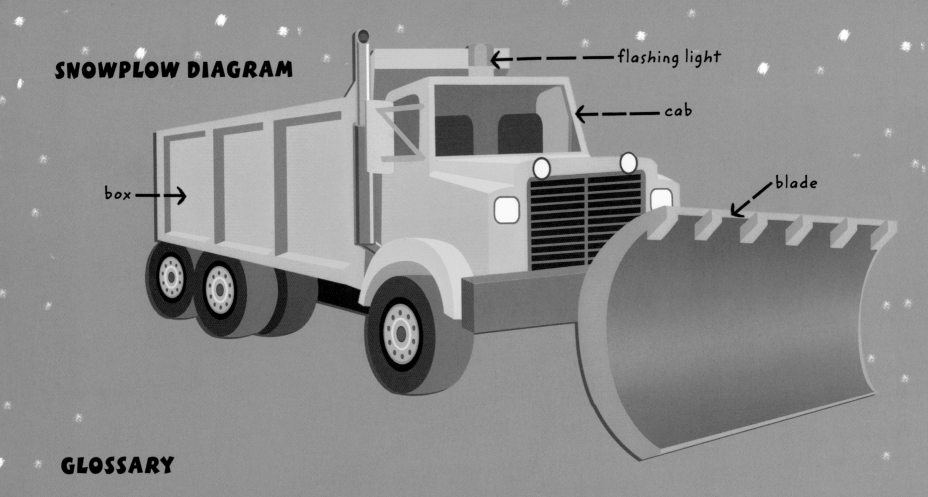

flashing light

cab

box

blade

GLOSSARY

blade—the wide part on the front of a snowplow that pushes the snow

box—the back of the truck that holds the salt and sand

cab—the front of the snowplow where the driver sits

joystick—a control stick next to the driver on a truck

lever—a bar or handle used to move the snowplow blade

spinners—the plastic disks on the back of a snowplow's box that spray the salt and sand over the road

22

FUN FACTS

 Most snowplow drivers know first aid. They are often the first to arrive at snowy accidents and may need to help injured people.

 Flags are often attached to the front corners of a snowplow's hood. This helps the driver see the front corners of the plow when snow makes it hard to see.

 Although each truck has just one driver, snowplow drivers often do their work in teams. This is called gang plowing.

 If a snowplow driver finds a car covered in snow, he or she puts orange cones around the car. This helps keep other plows from driving into it.

 Sometimes, snowplows are used to clear more than snow. When there is a lumber or gravel spill on the highway, snowplows can help clean up the mess.

23

TO LEARN MORE

At the Library

Patrick, Jean L.S. *If I Had a Snowplow.* Honesdale, Penn.: Boyds Mills Press, 2001.

Randolph, Joanne. *Snowplows.* New York: PowerKids Press, 2002.

Rogers, Hal. *Snowplows.* Chanhassen, Minn.: Child's World, 2001.

Sherman, Josepha. *Flakes and Flurries: A Book About Snow.* Minneapolis: Picture Window Books, 2004.

On the Web

FactHound offers a safe, fun way to find Web sites related to this book. All of the sites on FactHound have been researched by our staff. www.facthound.com

1. Visit the FactHound home page.

2. Enter a search word related to this book, or type in this special code: 1404806172.

3. Click on the FETCH IT button.

Your trusty FactHound will fetch the best Web sites for you!

INDEX

BOOKS IN THIS SERIES

- I Drive an Ambulance
- I Drive a Bulldozer
- I Drive a Dump Truck
- I Drive a Garbage Truck
- I Drive a Semitruck
- I Drive a Snowplow

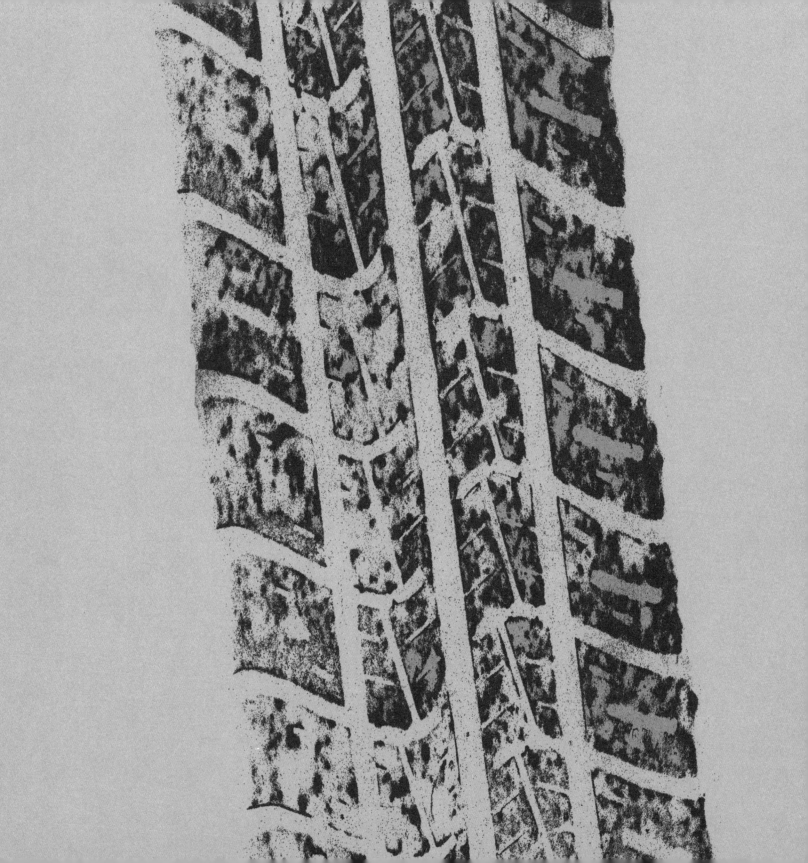